The
AUTOMOBILE COLLECTION
Heritage Plantation of Sandwich

FOREWORD

I believe it is most appropriate that this beautifully illustrated book describing the collection of antique and classic automobiles at Heritage Plantation of Sandwich should appear during the 100th anniversary year of the automobile. While there is some controversy about the actual centennial year, it is generally agreed that a German should be granted the credit for the invention. On January 29, 1886 a patent was issued to Carl Benz for the first vehicle powered by a gasoline-fueled, internal-combustion engine. This original 3-wheeled "Patent Motor Wagen" is now on display in the Deutsches Museum in Munich and bares little resemblance to today's sleek Mercedes-Benz.

What can be seen today in Heritage Plantation's Round Barn, a replica of the Shaker Round Barn in Hancock, Massachusetts, is often referred to as the most selective antique and classic car collection east of the Henry Ford Museum in Dearborn, Michigan. Nine of the ten best American cars picked for *Life* magazine in its September, 1983 cover story are represented in our 33-car collection. Six models are of the exact same year, three are basically the same models separated by one year and the tenth and only car missing is a much newer model than any of the cars in the Heritage collection.

It seems fitting that Massachusetts license plate "Antique Number One" is registered to a car in our collection, the 1909 White Steam Car, which was the first official automobile of a President of the United States. It was used by President Taft during his 1908-12 administration. While President Theodore Roosevelt had a car for his personal use before this, it was not an official presidential vehicle because only horse-drawn carriages had this designation up to that time.

In 1982, the Heritage Automobile Museum received another "Number One" distinction. Michelin Guide awarded the Museum its top three-star rating and wrote, "Restored to their original appearance, these mint-condition autos sparkle with their highly polished nickel and brass trim." To fully appreciate the significance of this rating, it should be noted that only eight other museums in New England, including Boston's Museum of Fine Arts, were awarded three stars at that time.

What follows is the story behind the Heritage Plantation automobile collection. During the winter of 1964, I visited Smoke Tree Ranch near Palm Springs, California, and could not believe my eyes when I saw a group of people dressed in turn-of-the-century clothes driving beautifully restored cars of that same period! The owners of the cars were Mr. and Mrs. Donald S. Gilmore of Kalamazoo, Michigan, who knew my family quite well because Mr. Gilmore was also in the business of manufacturing pharmaceuticals. They were extremely cordial and through them I learned the

names of the various clubs that are devoted to the preservation of antique automobiles. Before leaving California, I visited the home office of the Horseless Carriage Club and joined its membership. In its latest publication, I found an advertisement for a 1916 Crane-Simplex which was for sale in West Newton, Massachusetts, and went to see the car almost immediately after returning from California. This great old touring car became my first antique auto and may now be seen in its fully restored condition in the Round Barn. For me, the purchase of one antique car was the beginning of a search for more. The Crane-Simplex was followed by a toy-like beauty, a 1908 Waltham-Orient buckboard runabout built in Waltham, Massachusetts, the same year that Model T Fords went into production. This was followed by a partially restored world-famous Stutz Bearcat of 1915 vintage, built in my hometown of Indianapolis. Unable to find a wiring diagram for this car, we could not get it to run for some time. Finally one day a noise like thunder was heard from the garage — the Stutz had started! This was

due to the hard work and genius of two men, Carl Erickson and Elmer Bliss, both of whom were later to be employed by Heritage Plantation.

After this beginning the collection was expanded as rapidly as funds and garage space would allow, always aiming for outstanding cars in mint or at least restorable condition. When the collection reached thirty cars, an upgrading program was started — disposing of some that were not particularly outstanding and replacing them with better examples. In my mind some of the greatest "finds" were the Mercer Raceabout, the Duesenberg Tourster, the Auburn Boattail Speedster, and the Rolls-Royce Phaeton. The Rolls-Royce fits into our Americana theme because it was built in Springfield, Massachusetts, where Rolls-Royce had a branch plant from 1921 to 1935. The collection as it now stands is a representative cross section of American cars from their earliest days through the "classics" of the mid-1930's. It is by no means a complete cross section because of the literally hundreds of different makes of cars that have been built in America since 1893.

The idea of an automobile museum was always in the back of my mind, but as I became more and more involved with antique cars I came to realize that there were several other museums devoted just to this specialty, and it was questionable as to whether another one was needed. There was the very fine Museum of Transportation in Brookline, Massachusetts. The James Melton Museum in Florida had been an inspiration for a long time and when Melton died, I learned that a good many of his cars were purchased by Winthrop Rockefeller who started an antique car museum in Arkansas. The Rockefeller Museum did not last long and this further added to my doubts about an automobile museum as such. Then an event happened that started us all thinking in an entirely different vein as far as a museum was concerned.

I acquired my father's firearms and miniature soldier collections following his death. A nationally known collector, he was widely acclaimed as "The most retiring, unassuming collector of his generation and also among the greatest." With this inspiration, the idea of an automobile museum grew into the building of a diversified museum of Americana now known as Heritage Plantation of Sandwich, dedicated to the memory of my father, Josiah K. Lilly, Jr.

J. K. Lilly III

Josiah K. Lilly III

INTRODUCTION

O ne hundred years have now passed since the first motorcars appeared in Europe and began to take shape in the minds of American inventors. The automobile was the product of a few farsighted individuals who sought more efficient ways to transport people and goods than were provided by horse-drawn vehicles. To the more conservative element, the new invention was at first a noisy and unwelcome arrival. For many others, it was a novelty considered to be a plaything for the less practical or more adventurous members of society.

Eventually, when the "horseless carriage" proved to be an efficient product and when mass production made it more obtainable, the automobile became a way of life to countless thousands. The motor car was

soon America's most popular means of transportation as well as one of its chief symbols of affluence, achievement, engineering skill and aesthetic perfection.

The enormous popularity of the new mechanical wonder resulted in more than 2,200 manufacturers in the United States alone undertaking to design, produce and market automobiles. This led to the growth of numerous related businesses and occupations including oil refining, tire manufacturing, road construction and service station operation to name just a few.

A changing economy and fierce competition forced many car builders to cease operation, but their products live on in legend and story. These tales of the legacy of the automobile industry have aroused the

curiosity of present generations, resulting in the keen desire of many to learn more about the automobile's past. At the same time advances in technology combined with changes in design, and unfortunately what many consider a decline in the quality of construction, have evoked a nostalgia for the "good old days" among those who still remember driving a speeding Mercer or riding in a rumble seat.

With the growing interest in the history of the motor car, Heritage Plantation of Sandwich is exceptionally proud and pleased to have the unique ability to display and interpret its magnificent Josiah K. Lilly III automobile collection. The collection is a tribute to Mr. Lilly's desire to keep a vital

the Museum's Automobile Curator,
G. Robert Melber, written by David Brownell,
antique auto editor, collector and historian,
and with color photography by Alan Hudson,
it offers informative and factual texts as well
as exciting photographic interpretations of
each of the American-made cars exhibited in
our award winning Round Barn Automobile
Museum.

Gene A. Schott, Director

segment of American history alive. It is also
a testimonial to his skill in selecting the
finest examples of both engineering achievement and excellence of design.

As a special project to commemorate the
100th anniversary of the motorcar, we are
delighted to have been afforded the
opportunity to publish this catalogue of the
Heritage collection. Under the direction of

THE ROUND STONE BARN

Eric Sloane's captivating painting of the Round Stone Barn in Shaker Village, Hancock, Massachusetts, inspired our trustees to envision this unique design as ideal for exhibiting the Josiah K. Lilly III automobile collection documented in this catalogue. The functionality of this concept reflects the Shaker tradition of efficient simplicity popularized today by reproductions of their totally utilitarian yet singularly beautiful furniture.

The Shakers were a celibate, communal society which developed in England, and set sail for the United States in the 1770's. They reached their maximum population of 6000 during the 19th century in numerous settlements mostly in the northeastern part of this country. Growth of the Shaker sect depended solely upon the adoption of families whose beliefs were in concert with the Shakers' strict religious principles.

The original Round Stone Barn, ninety feet in diameter, was built in 1826 to house 52 dairy cattle kept in pie-shaped stalls arranged around the periphery of the ground floor. The center circle served as the hay mow supplied from horsedrawn wagons driven around the upper level of the building. The original barn was rebuilt in 1865, following a disastrous fire, and a twelve-sided superstructure, or monitor, was added in the 1870's to greatly increase the limited ventilation and illumination previously provided only by the cupola and a few windows.

The Heritage Round Stone Barn, finished in Connecticut shale and siding salvaged from old New England structures, is 96 feet in diameter. Its center roof-support timbers stand 38 feet tall from ground level to the pinnacle, capped by the octagonal 12 foot high cupola. This beautiful structure presents to our visitors a two-level panoramic view of the Heritage collection. Unique for auto museums, the fact that the cars are not roped off permits the viewer to further appreciate the beauty of each car in close-up detail.

G. Robert Melber, Curator

SPECIFICATIONS

Price new: $600
Engine: Four cylinder flat head configuration, 3¾″ x 4″ bore and stroke, 20 horsepower
Wheelbase: 100 inches
Transmission: Planetary, foot actuated, two speeds forward, one reverse
Manufacturer: Ford Motor Company, Detroit, Mich. (1903-present)

1913 Ford Touring

enry Ford didn't invent the automobile. In fact, there is not one "invention" of Henry Ford's in the Model T. Virtually every feature of the car had been developed by other companies and individuals prior to the T's introduction on October 1, 1908. Henry Ford's gift was the ability to take these disparate elements from various cars and blend them into a tough, basic, reliable, economical automobile. Or, as old Henry himself defined it, a "universal car."

So much myth and nonsense have been perpetuated about the doughty Model T that a few facts on this remarkable car are needed for a fair and balanced view.

Fact: The Model T indeed put the world on self-propelled wheels, with over 15 million examples being built between 1908 and 1927, a production record only recently surpassed by the VW "beetle".

Fact: By 1920, every other car in the world was a Model T.

Fact: By 1923, Ford's production efficiencies had brought the base price of a T roadster down to $290.

Fact: Until 1914 Model T's could be ordered in a relative rainbow of colors. The "any color as long as it's black" policy came in with the development of quick-drying soybean-based paint.

Fact: The planetary transmission works on the same basic principles as the modern-day automatic transmission, the essential difference being that the shifting is actuated by the driver's feet in the T and by hydraulic pressure in a modern car.

The Heritage Model T touring is one of the most popular cars in the Round Barn because visitors can actually touch, feel and sit in it, imagining what motoring in 1913 felt like.

SPECIFICATIONS
Price new: $975
Engine: Lycoming straight eight flat head configuration, 3" x 4¾" bore and stroke, 100 horsepower
Wheelbase: 127 inches
Transmission: Selective three speeds forward, one reverse with free wheeling in conjunction with Columbia dual ratio rear axle
Manufacturer: Auburn Automobile Co., Auburn, Ind. (1900-1936).

1932 Auburn Boattail Speedster

ounded in 1900 by successful carriage manufacturers Frank and Morris Eckhart, the first production Auburn car hit the streets in 1903. Through the pioneer years of motoring and until the early 1920's, Auburns enjoyed moderate success and a good reputation as dependable, attractive automobiles.

However, by 1923 Auburn, like many old-line independent manufacturers, was being squeezed by the fierce competition among the major automakers and was teetering near failure. Unlike most companies of the time though, Auburn was rescued and the rescuer was one of the most remarkable characters in American auto history: Erret Lobban Cord.

Cord proved to be the *wunderkind* of the U.S. auto industry. By turning Auburn into a high quality car at a remarkably low price, he built the financial base to acquire Duesenberg and Lycoming Engine Company and to launch a radical, beautiful front wheel drive car bearing his own name.

In 1931 a new, sleekly styled line of Auburn eight cylinder cars was introduced, followed in 1932 by a spectacular V-12 powered line of cars, some of which were pegged to sell for less than $1,000! The stunning 1931-32 cars, designed by Al Leamy who was also the stylist of the Cord L-29, were refined versions of the Auburn boattail speedsters first offered in 1928.

Beyond their smashing good looks Auburns offered a raft of standard features which were found only on costlier cars. These included a two-speed rear end and the then-popular free wheeling, Bijur automatic chassis lubrication, Lovejoy adjustable shock absorbers and Startix automatic re-start.

Heritage Plantation's 1932 Auburn model 8-100A Speedster is regarded by many visitors as the most beautiful car in the collection. With its silver and black livery, sharply pointed boattail, narrow luxurious cockpit, long hood and graceful flowing fender line, it is the epitome of Depression-era optimism and glamour: virtually a four-wheeled movie star.

69.6.2

SPECIFICATIONS
Price new: $7,500 (chassis only $4,250)
Engine: Four-cylinder Knight patent sleeve
  valve configuration, 4″ x 5½″ bore and
  stroke, 30 horsepower
Wheelbase: 125 inches
Transmission: Selective three speeds forward,
  one reverse
Manufacturer: Brewster & Co.,
  Long Island City, N.Y. (1915-1925)

1916 Brewster Town Landaulet

Produced by the venerable Brewster coachbuilding firm from 1915 through 1925, these elegant, understated motorcars were built for wealthy clients on a bespoke basis. They were considered an excellent choice for town and city use thanks to the smooth and relatively silent sleeve valve engine.

Brewsters were offered in both closed and open body styles and were recognizable through their distinctive oval radiator shape.

Production, always miniscule, came to a total halt when Brewster was bought by Rolls-Royce of America, Inc. to become Rolls-Royce's ''captive'' coachbuilder. Previously, Brewster had been Rolls-Royce of America's leading contractor for custom coachwork on their Springfield, Mass.-built chassis.

The Brewster automobile name was revived briefly from 1934 to 1936 when approximately 300 cars, many using distinctive heart-shaped grilles conceived by Brewster, were produced on Ford, Buick and other standard U.S. chassis.

The Heritage Plantation Brewster is in totally original condition and demonstrates the high order of materials and

workmanship which went into these cars. Many Brewsters, like the car on display, carried such fillips as intricate canework on the body, leather fenders in the tradition of fine carriages, and beautifully appointed interiors complete with speaking tube for passenger to chauffeur conversation.

69.6.3

SPECIFICATIONS

Price new: $1,795 with top
Engine: Four cylinder, individually cast configuration, 4¼″ x 4½″ bore and stroke, 33 horsepower
Wheelbase: 110 inches
Transmission: Selective three speeds forward, one reverse
Manufacturer: Cadillac Motor Car Co., Detroit, Mich. (1903-present)

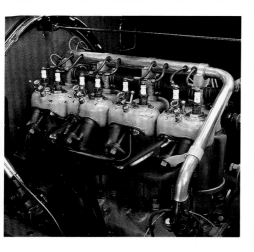

1910 Cadillac Model 30 Roadster

Successful from its start in 1903, Cadillac was the brainchild of Henry M. Leland whose precision machine work and manufacturing standardization techniques were renowned before he ever built his own car.

Further accolades for Leland's effective interchangability program came in 1908 from England's Royal Automobile Club. Three one-cylinder Cadillacs were completely disassembled, their parts scrambled and the cars reassembled by the British distributor's mechanics, using simple hand tools.

This "Standardization Test," performed under the critical gaze of club officials included, after reassembly of the three little cars, a 500-mile full throttle reliability run around the then-new Brooklands racing oval. All three cars performed flawlessly, much to the astonishment of many of the English skeptics, and Cadillac was duly awarded the prestigious Dewar Trophy for their unparalleled performances. This was the automotive equivalent of winning the Nobel Prize.

From this successful range of cars, Cadillac went on its innovative way as the pioneer U.S. firm to introduce an electric starting and lighting system, a volume-produced V-8 engine, synchromesh

transmission and their own mighty, memorable versions of V-12 and V-16 engines.

The Heritage collection's 1910 Cadillac roadster is an unusual body style because this model was vastly outsold by the five passenger touring car. Also unusual is the little roadster's double "mother-in-law" folding seat at the rear of its body.

SPECIFICATIONS

Price new: $6,900
Engine: Sixteen cylinders in two banks of eight each, overhead valve configuration, 3″ x 4″ bore and stroke, 165 horsepower
Wheelbase: 148 inches
Transmission: Selective three speeds forward, one reverse with synchromesh second and third gears
Manufacturer: Cadillac Motor Car Co., Detroit, Mich. (1903-present)

1930 Cadillac V-16 Convertible Coupe

No less a personage than the great British auto engineer and designer W.O. Bentley described his test drive in a Cadillac V-16 thusly: "My chief memories of this automobile (although that term is inadequate) were its astonishing refinement with perhaps the most completely successful elimination of evidence that explosions were occurring under the bonnet ever obtained in a motor car. The word 'torque' also took on a new meaning with this V-16. . ."

Indeed, Cadillac's V-16 was a mechanical tour de force of jovian proportions and Bentley, a man hardly given to overstatement, had gotten the characteristics of this remarkable powerhouse exactly right.

Cadillac's introduction of these mammoth motorcars during the onset of the Great Depression might seem the height of folly at first blush. But sheer profit wasn't the motive with the V-16 and companion V-12 cars. The objective instead was to snatch the prestige car crown from arch-rival Packard, and Cadillac's scheme succeeded to some good extent, making inroads at the top of the luxury market.

The Heritage collection's V-16 carries a Fleetwood custom body, as do most of these cars, since Fleetwood was General Motors' "in-house" custom coachworks. This beautiful car carries such amenities as a small door each side for golf clubs, arm rests in the rumble seat which has an interior release for security, and mahogany strips on the running boards and the trunk rack.

The car has a prodigious appetite for fuel, averaging 4½ mpg in normal driving.

Cadillac's early V-16's are considered by many classic car connoisseurs to be among the very best automobiles ever built in America, and the equal of any contemporary from overseas as well.

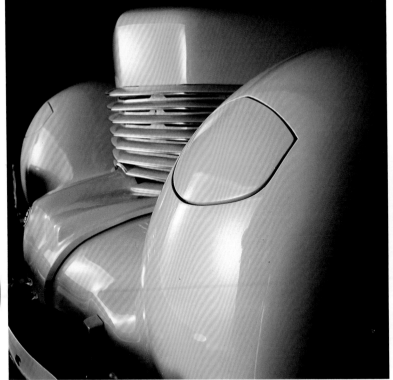

SPECIFICATIONS
Price new: $2,645
Engine: Lycoming flat head V-8 configuration, 3½″ x 3¾″ bore and stroke, 125 horsepower
Wheelbase: 125 inches
Transmission: Four speeds forward, one reverse, activated by a Bendix preselector mechanism with shifting effected through electric solenoids and engine vacuum
Manufacturer: Auburn Automobile Co., Auburn, Ind. (1929-1937)

1937 Cord 812 Phaeton

riginally conceived as a "compact," lower-priced Duesenberg, the Cord 810 appeared in late 1935, marking a revival of the Cord name among auto nameplates. It had been dormant since the end of 1931 when production of the elegant, front wheel drive Cord L-29 ceased.

Regarded as the most striking and aesthetically successful U.S. car from the mid-1930's, Gordon Buehrig's masterful design bristled with innovations like disappearing headlamps, the total elimination of running boards, "alligator" style hood opening and "coffin nose" front end styling which would influence other makes in years ahead. Wedded to this were a front wheel drive system considerably improved from its L-29 predecessor, and in 1937, the option of a supercharged engine.

These second generation Cords were rushed to production after a triumphant reception at auto shows throughout the country. Despite some teething problems, including a tendency for the early cars to overheat and suffer transmission glitches, demand for these sleek, chic automobiles remained steady throughout their short life.

Contrary to some claims, neither the Cord's price nor its radical engineering caused its demise. Rather, the main reason was E. L. Cord's desire to expand his empire toward defense contracts for the war he was convinced would come soon and disrupt all auto making in America, not just his beautiful four-wheeled namesakes.

Whether the Cord 810/812 was a mechanical success or failure is really irrelevant. As a design, it is as pleasing to the eye as it was when first seen by the world over 50 years ago. And how many cars can claim that distinction?

SPECIFICATIONS
Price new: $750
Engine: Four cylinder flat head configuration,
   3¾" x 4" bore and stroke, 20 horsepower
Wheelbase: 100 inches
Transmission: Planetary, foot actuated,
   two speeds forward, one reverse
Manufacturer: Ford Motor Company,
   Detroit, Mich. (1903-present)

1915 Ford Couplet

he Couplet body style is an especially scarce one on the Model T as it was offered only from 1915 to 1917, and at $750 in 1915 was one of the most expensive Model T's ever built.

Mechanically, the car is identical to all other Model T's. Its distinction lies in its "convertible" bodywork.

This Couplet is one of the Collection's most traveled cars, having originally been owned by multimillionaire Sir Talbot Ewart, an Irish Earl. It served as the nobleman's honeymoon car and when his wife died only three years after their marriage, the little Ford was put on blocks with just 4200 miles on it and never turned a wheel under Sir Talbot's guidance again.

This Model T sports an accessory Sears Cross Co. speedometer which reads to 60 mph, and an odometer for both total and trip mileage.

The 1915 Fords represent a curious blend of the old and the new. Their brass radiators were an antiquated sight by 1915 and used on no other cars. But alongside the radiator is the latest in lighting. However, since Fords had no battery system the lights got their power from the magneto, becoming progressively brighter as engine speed increased until finally the bulbs would blow, leaving the hapless 1915 Ford driver literally in the dark.

17

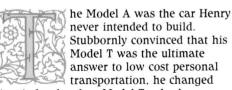

SPECIFICATIONS

Price new: $580
Engine: Four cylinder flat head configuration, $3^7/_8$" x $4^1/_4$" bore and stroke, 40 horsepower
Wheelbase: $103^1/_2$ inches
Transmission: Selective three speeds forward, one reverse
Manufacturer: Ford Motor Company, Detroit, Mich. (1903-present)

1931 Ford Deluxe Phaeton

The Model A was the car Henry never intended to build. Stubbornly convinced that his Model T was the ultimate answer to low cost personal transportation, he changed his mind only when Model T sales became drastically squeezed by flashier, more modern competition, with Chevrolet the toughest rival.

Shutting his factories for nearly a year, he concentrated on developing the T's worthy successor. So powerful was Ford's grip on the motoring public that this hiatus in Ford production put a severe kink in competitors' sales, while America waited for "the new Ford."

When the Model A arrived in showrooms in December, 1927 the dealers were mobbed. The new Ford looked like a smaller version of the Lincoln, and while retaining evergreen Model T features like transverse springs, it boasted a "regular" transmission and clutch, four wheel brakes, a powerful, simple engine with twice the horsepower of its predecessor and safety glass. Initially, demand for the Model A far overwhelmed even Ford's vast production capabilities. More than four million of them would eventually be built before Ford introduced his third great automotive advance, the V-8 engine of 1932.

During the A's production span a wide variety of body styles, from fundamental pickup truck to formal town car, were offered on its rugged chassis. Among them, the Deluxe two-door Phaeton is exclusive to the 1930-31 model years and was one of the most expensive Ford offerings of those times. It was a scarce sight even when new with just 2,229 built during 1931, and the Heritage collection's car is one of the few examples of this attractive body style extant today.

SPECIFICATIONS

Price new: $2,750
Engine: Air-cooled six cylinder overhead valve configuration, 3¼″ x 4″ bore and stroke, 32 horsepower
Wheelbase: 119 inches
Transmission: Selective three speeds forward, one reverse
Manufacturer: Franklin Automobile Co., Syracuse, N.Y. (1901-1934)

1925 Franklin Sport Runabout

Until the ubiquitous Volkswagen "beetle" came along, Franklin was the most successful air-cooled car in history.

From its beginnings in 1901 Franklin was an innovative automaker. Its first cars used an engine set cross-ways in the chassis, exactly like many small modern cars. And Franklin stuck with its trademark air-cooling right to the end in 1934, leaving the automotive scene with a spectacular V-12 engine powering its most costly and beautiful cars.

In between time Franklin built a steady stream of four and then six cylinder cars. They were usually more renowned for their reliability, craftsmanship and superb riding qualities, thanks to a laminated wood frame and full elliptic springs, than for their stylish appearance.

Franklin changed that image in 1925, however, with a newly designed line of cars which were a total departure from previous body styles. These new cars, designed by the exceptionally talented J. Frank de Causse, one of America's first true automotive stylists, featured razor-edge, angular bodies a large false radiator to give the appearanc of a water-cooled car and gracefully integrated fenders. Though the styling was controversial within the company, the proo was in the showroom and these Series II cars caused Franklin sales to soar like the airplanes they likened their engineering to. Among all these, though, surely the boat-tailed runabout as seen in the Heritage collection had to be the most attractive, bot in the showroom and on the roads of the roaring twenties.

SPECIFICATIONS

Price new: $3,250
Engine: Four cylinder overhead valve configuration, 5″ x 4¾″ bore and stroke, 40 horsepower
Wheelbase: 117 inches
Transmission: Selective three speeds forward, one reverse
Manufacturer: Knox Automobile Co., Springfield, Mass. (1900-1914)

1910 Knox Model R Touring

 echanically gifted Harry A. Knox was working at the Overman Wheel Co. of Chicopee Falls, Mass. in the late 1890's when he turned out three experimental gasoline-powered cars for that firm. Mr. Overman, however, thought steam cars were the coming thing, so Knox left to form his own company which began producing winsome air-cooled three wheeled runabouts in 1900. Four wheelers became part of Knox's offerings in 1902, and all cars used the so-called "porcupine" air cooling principle which depended on two-inch pins sticking out of the cylinder barrels, rather than the more usual fins, to direct air onto the engine.

These engines apparently worked very well and the Knox was advertised as "The Car That Never Drinks."

In 1904 Knox again made a sudden move, leaving the company he founded to build air-cooled and later sleeve-valve Atlas cars in Springfield.

By 1908 the Knox had evolved into a medium priced car which offered both water and air-cooled power plants and by 1910, when the Heritage collection's beautifully restored Knox hit the road for the first time, water cooling was used exclusively. A particularly unique feature in this impressive automobile is the swivel design of the two "jump seats," providing added comfort for five rear passengers.

A six cylinder car was part of the 1911 and subsequent model line, and the company had a brief fling at big-time racing in events like the Indianapolis 500 which failed, however, to bring the hoped-for sales results. Meanwhile, the cars kept growing larger and increasingly expensive in a field being dominated by more advanced and prestigious names. Manufacture of the Knox automobile was quietly dropped in 1914.

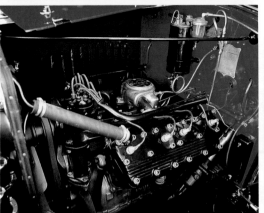

SPECIFICATIONS

Price new: $2,995
Engine: V-8 flat head configuration,
  $3\frac{1}{8}''$ x $4\frac{15}{16}''$ bore and stroke, 75 horsepower
Wheelbase: 125 inches
Transmission: Selective three speeds forward,
  one reverse
Manufacturer: Cadillac Motor Car Co.,
  Detroit, Mich. (1927-1940)

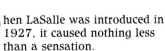

1927 LaSalle Sport Phaeton

When LaSalle was introduced in 1927, it caused nothing less than a sensation.

Designed by Harley Earl, General Motors' first chief stylist, as a chic companion car to Cadillac, the sibling nearly over-shadowed the parent with its sleek body styling, Hispano-Suiza-inspired radiator shape, attractive prices and solid Cadillac engineering.

After the successful debut, LaSalle continued its popular rise among upscale motorists until the Depression struck, breaking the marque's momentum and rising sales. By 1933, General Motors executives were seriously considering dropping the name and carrying on with Cadillac alone.

Once again, Harley Earl and his staff came to the rescue by changing the market and the personality of the car with a radical restyling for 1934, as sensational as the 1927 offering had been. The car was changed to straight eight power, prices were slashed boldly and sales improved. LaSalle acquired V-8 power again in 1937 and

finally vanished after the 1940 model year, having done its job of helping to carry Cadillac through some quite lean times.

The Heritage collection's LaSalle is an especially attractive one. Its dual cowl body style was rare even in 1927, with only ten of this particularly beautiful model having been built. It is believed that the other nine are no longer in existence.

SPECIFICATIONS

Price new: $4,600
Engine: V-8 flat head configuration, 3½″ x 5″ bore and stroke, 90 horsepower
Wheelbase: 136 inches
Transmission: Selective three speeds forward, one reverse
Manufacturer: Lincoln Motor Co., Detroit, Mich. (1920-present).

1927 Lincoln Sport Touring

hen Ford Motor Company purchased fledgling, failing Lincoln from Henry M. Leland in 1922, they acquired a car that would need virtually no mechanical changes for nearly ten years, so well had Cadillac founder Leland engineered the Lincoln marque right from its 1920 beginnings.

What Lincoln did get from Ford's ownership was improved body styling, something it badly needed to compete in the burgeoning luxury car market of the affluent twenties. Its stolid, stodgy styling quickly evolved into an attractive, distinctive line of custom and semi-custom-bodied cars by America's leading coachbuilders.

Its appeal cut across all segments of society. With its powerful engine and rugged, good handling chassis, the Lincoln quickly became popular among rumrunners and the police departments who pursued them, while also becoming a dominant part of the official White House fleet starting in 1924 during the Coolidge administration.

The Heritage collection's Lincoln carries a custom seven-passenger body by Locke and Co. of Rochester, N.Y. An early version of the modern "tilt" steering wheel is found on this Lincoln. Called a "fat man's wheel," it pivots out of the way to allow easier access and exit to and from the driver's seat. The graceful Greyhound radiator mascot's design is supposed to have been ordered by Edsel Ford. He was also responsible for bringing Lincoln the style and prestige it enjoyed throughout the 1920's and 1930's, culminating in the memorable Lincoln Continental introduced in 1940.

27

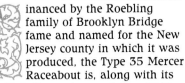

SPECIFICATIONS

Price new: $2,500
Engine: Four cylinder T-head configuration, $4^3/_8''$ x $5''$ bore and stroke, 58 horsepower
Wheelbase: 108 inches
Transmission: Selective four speeds forward, one reverse
Top speed: 70-plus miles per hour
Manufacturer: Mercer Automobile Co., Trenton, N.J. (1910-1925)

1912 Mercer Raceabout

Financed by the Roebling family of Brooklyn Bridge fame and named for the New Jersey county in which it was produced, the Type 35 Mercer Raceabout is, along with its arch-rival Stutz Bearcat, one of America's premier antique cars.

Designed by Finley R. Porter, an engineering genius from Long Island, the T-head Mercer packs tire-burning wallop, thanks to a superb power-to-weight ratio and the use of top quality components and construction techniques throughout. The transmission gears, for instance, are carried on ball rather than plain bearings, an advanced and costly practice which results in a shifting action so smooth and precise that double-clutching is not required!

One look at the Heritage collection's Mercer demonstrates why the name "Raceabout" is so apt. Weather protection is nonexistent save for the "monocle" windshield for the driver. It manages to keep the larger bugs away from one's face. Two minimal bucket seats bolt to the floor. Behind them is a large bolster tank for the fuel and a turtle-deck trunk just big enough for a tool kit and a change of clothes. Up front, a small, rounded cowl perches almost parallel with the strapped-down hood. The throttle pedal mounts outside the cowl like a saddle stirrup so the wind whistles up the driver's right leg. Fenders, running boards and lighting equipment remove easily for rapid conversion to a full-fledged racing car without further modification or adjustments. No wonder the Mercer has been called America's first sports car.

On top of all that there was the factory guarantee, unheard of in 1912, that each Raceabout would achieve a minimum 70 mph in stock form on public roads! This is a time when most cars had trouble seeing the far side of 40 mph.

During 1915, after myriad successes on tracks and roads throughout America, the T-head Raceabout was supplanted by a more modern Mercer with semi-enclosed coachwork and an L-head four cylinder engine. While thoroughly modern for 1915, the new design lacked the visceral appeal of its predecessor. After surviving several fiscal crises, a change of ownership and continually dwindling sales, the illustrious Mercer marque ceased production in 1925. An attempt was made to revive the name in

1930-31 but this effort died in the prototype stage after one car and one other chassis had been produced.

The Heritage collection's Mercer, like a number of the Raceabouts, has had an interesting history of ownership. Among its previous owners was the late Ken Purdy, one of America's most prominent automotive writers, who tells of the car's discovery in Canada and his eventual purchase of it in his classic book, *Kings of the Road*. Purdy believed the car had a racing history and original ownership by Barney Oldfield, America's best known early-day racing driver. The car was acquired for the collection from a Massachusetts owner.

SPECIFICATIONS

Price new: $1,485
Motor: General Electric, powered by seven 6-volt batteries. (Originally powered by battery of 20 cells, Philadelphia, with rated charge of 180 ampere hours.)
Cruising range: 60-75 miles on a single charge
Top speed: 20 miles per hour
Wheelbase: 100 inches
Manufacturer: Milburn Wagon Co., Toledo, Ohio (1914-1923)

1915 Milburn Light Electric

uilt from 1914 to 1923, Milburn was one of the more successful makes of electric automobiles with over 7,000 examples sold through their production span.

One of Milburn's best customers was the U.S. Secret Service during President Woodrow Wilson's term. The silent-running electrics were perfectly suited to parade work as well as providing an unobtrusive "tail" for the first family. However, electric cars, Milburns included, never were a match for the speed and acceleration of gasoline cars. Their limited range on a full charge of the batteries vexes even some of the best engineers today, who see a use for electric cars in tomorrow's transportation mix.

The Milburn, with its elegant and airy interior, simple and quick tiller steering and two pedal controls was descended from the Ohio Electric, which was built in the Milburn works in 1909.

In 1919 Milburn management, very likely sensing that the telephone booth appearance of their cars was limiting their appeal, introduced two models designed to resemble contemporary gasoline-powered cars. They were less than successful in finding new customers for Milburn and were quickly and quietly dropped from the company's line.

By the early 1920's the popularity of the simple, silent, easily-operated but slow and limited electric automobile was nearly gone, taking the Milburn venture along with it.

The Milburn in the Heritage collection has been repainted and reupholstered in authentic color and material schemes.

SPECIFICATIONS

Price new: $1,300
Engine: Horizontally-opposed longitudinally-mounted two cylinder configuration, 4¾" x 4½" bore and stroke, 7 horsepower
Wheelbase: 69 inches
Transmission: Selective three speeds forward, one reverse
Manufacturer: J. Stevens Arms & Tool Co., Chicopee Falls, Mass. (1901-1906); The Stevens-Duryea Co., Chicopee Falls, Mass. (1906-1927)

1903 Stevens-Duryea Runabout

 he Duryea brothers have been credited with building in 1893 America's first successful vehicle powered by a gasoline-fueled, internal-combustion engine.

Pioneer auto developer, J. Frank Duryea, joined forces with Stevens Arms in 1901 through a merger with his Hampden Automobile & Launch Company. The Stevens-Duryea car resulted from this alliance.

The firm started with small but mechanically sophisticated runabouts. Sales literature for the little cars touted that "It starts from the seat" by means of a short crank attached to the steering post center-mounted in the driver's seat, adding that "A boy of eight readily starts one of these machines." The Model L in the Heritage collection is an excellent example of these earliest years.

Stevens-Duryea added two more cylinders to their cars in 1905 and in 1906 entered the luxury market with a 50 horsepower six cylinder model priced at $5000. They would continue to stay in the high-priced bracket until the end, building cars of impeccable quality and workmanship but with diminishing popularity as innovation in the early years gave way to design and engineering stagnation from the 'teens onward.

The company had closed down in January, 1915 for lack of working capital and its plant was sold to Westinghouse for war work. After the Armistice, the firm was revived by a Ray S. Deering and his associates who guaranteed exclusivity for the marque by jumping prices to the $10,000 range.

By the spring of 1922, thanks to spectacular mismanagement, Stevens-Duryea was again in the soup. This time receivership lasted 14 months. Reorganized once again under new management, production such as it was, resumed in January, 1924 and staggered along until 1927 when one of the finest motorcars ever built in New England finally joined the growing ranks of automotive has-beens.

SPECIFICATIONS

Price new: $650
Engine: One cylinder, horizontal configuration, 5″ x 6″ bore and stroke, 7 horsepower
Wheelbase: 66 inches
Transmission: Planetary, two speeds forward, one reverse
Manufacturer: Olds Motor Works, now Oldsmobile Division of General Motors, Lansing, Michigan (1896-present)

1904 Oldsmobile Runabout

The Model T Ford may have put America on wheels, but Olds could certainly lay claim that the curved dash runabout put many Americans into their first car.

From 1903 through 1905, Oldsmobile produced more cars than any other U.S. manufacturer — 5.508 in 1904 alone, which is more than triple Ford's production for that year. Oldsmobile continues today as America's oldest name in the automotive world.

First built in 1901, the curved dash Olds was a clever, sturdy design. Despite its light weight and diminutive wheelbase, it rode easily thanks to the long, single fore-to-aft springs on each side of the car. Performance was more than adequate too, thanks to a favorable power-to-weight ratio. The Olds was attractively priced and its durability and reliability proven by a successful San Francisco to New York trek in one of the little cars in 1903.

Even with Oldsmobile's introduction of larger and more powerful cars beginning in 1904, the distinctive, ubiquitous curved dash runabouts were available until 1908 and are highly popular today among collectors of early cars.

The Heritage collection's beautifully restored curved dash Oldsmobile is painted in the standard color scheme of black with red trim.

SPECIFICATIONS

Price new: $3,500
Engine: Four cylinder T-head configuration, cast in pairs, 5″ x 6″ bore and stroke, 40 horsepower
Wheelbase: 126 inches
Transmission: Selective four speeds forward, one reverse
Manufacturer: Olds Motor Works, Lansing, Mich. (1896-present)

1912 Oldsmobile Autocrat Roadster

Nothing could present a greater contrast in the same make of cars than this long and husky speedster and its predecessor curved dash runabout.

In the years 1905-1915, American auto development took dramatic leaps forward . . . and sideways. This brass-festooned sports car reflects the quest for speed, power and endurance sought by most makers at that time.

Almost everything about the Autocrat roadster is larger than life. The engine holds 12 quarts of oil, the gasoline tanks 40 gallons of fuel. Cooling is achieved by 28 quarts of water. The wheels are three feet in diameter. Springing is supplemented by friction shock absorbers.

Yet, this was not Oldsmobile's largest offering during those days. That honor belongs to the gargantuan Limited series: a six cylinder, 60 horsepower model of 140 inch wheelbase, a tire size of 42 x 4½ inches, and a list price of $5,000 to $7,000 depending upon the body style.

These wonderful, inefficient monsters were too expensive even for those tax-free times. By 1916 no Oldsmobile cost more than $1,850, horsepower was down to as little as 30, and Olds had established itself as one of the pillars of General Motors.

The Heritage collection's superbly restored Autocrat is an outstanding example of a great early-day sports car.

SPECIFICATIONS

Price new: $9,500 (chassis only)
Engine: Straight eight, overhead valve configuration actuated by dual overhead camshafts, four valves per cylinder, 3¾″ x 4¾″ bore and stroke, 265 horsepower
Wheelbase: 153½ inches (or 142½″ at option of customer)
Transmission: Selective three speeds forward, one reverse
Manufacturer: Duesenberg, Inc., Indianapolis, Ind. (1920-1937)

1930 Duesenberg Model J Derham Tourster

ore superlatives—and more fanciful legends—are showered upon the Model J Duesenberg than on any other American car.

Understandably so. From the moment it burst upon the luxury car scene in late 1928, through the grim Depression, to today when it is the most coveted and costly of all U.S.-built classic cars, the Duesy seems larger than life itself.

A look at some specifications reveals why it is held in such awe. The Model J engine holds 12 quarts of oil, its cooling system 28 quarts of water, the gasoline tank 26 gallons of fuel.

The most illustrious designers and coachbuilders of the time lavished their talent and artistry on the J's chassis, resulting in some of the most memorable motorcars ever to turn a wheel. And while certainly handsome in enclosed body styles, it seemed that the more rakish and open the body the better it suited the Duesenberg's powerhouse of a chassis.

For here was a car which developed better than six and one-half times the horsepower of a contemporary Model A Ford, two and one-half times that of the most expensive Packard, and one hundred more horses than the rival Cadillac V-16! To top things off in the horsepower department, a supercharger option introduced in 1932 boosted the brake horsepower output on the Duesy to a heady 320!

For the fortunate driver of this king of the road the instrument panel provided a complete range of information, some of which was previously encountered only in an

aircraft. Besides the 150 mph speedometer and 5000 rpm tachometer there were, among other niceties, a split second chronograph, an altimeter, brake pressure gauge and service warning lights to signal when an oil change was due or the battery water was low!

The Model J Duesenberg was another brainchild of super-entrepreneur E.L. Cord. It was the embodiment of his ambition to build the most fabulous car in the world in terms of performance and luxury. He had acquired the faltering Duesenberg firm in 1926 and with it the considerable talents of Fred and August Duesenberg, two German-born Iowa farm boys blessed with an abundance of natural mechanical aptitude.

Their combined talents had resulted in a series of innovative racing cars and engines, marine motors and aircraft engines for WWI fighters. The early 1920's saw the Duesenbergs building passenger cars of exceptional performance, as well as competition cars which won the French Grand Prix and a number of Indy 500 contests, prior to their firm's rescue by Cord.

Thanks to their price, appearance and reputation the J Duesenbergs attracted some notable patronage both here and abroad. Flamboyant New York Mayor Jimmy Walker owned a Duesenberg, as did film greats

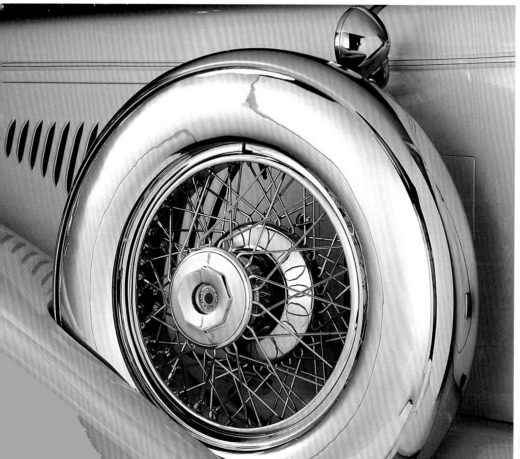

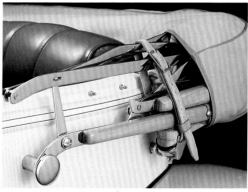

Tyrone Power and Clark Gable, comedian Joe E. Brown, the elusive Greta Garbo, newspaper tycoon William Randolph Hearst, King Alfonso of Spain, Prince Nicholas of Roumania, the redoubtable Prince Sahibzada Nawod Azum of Hyderabad and, one of the best-known owners of all, Gary Cooper, whose Duesenberg is the star of the Heritage collection.

This car is one of only eight Derham Toursters ever produced, and the first one sold. Some Duesenberg connoisseurs consider it to be the most graceful and attractive of all the touring car body styles. It certainly represents one of the many high points in the career of the gifted Gordon Buehrig, who would go on to design other memorable Duesenberg bodies as well as the Cord 810/812 and several other classics.

The Heritage Model J is restored in its original color scheme of primrose yellow and parkway green, just as it appeared on the floor of the Los Angeles Salon in 1930 where it was purchased by the great movie star.

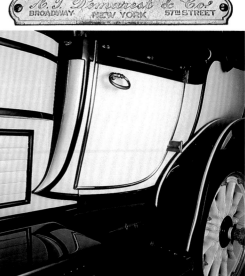

SPECIFICATIONS

Price new: Unknown due to custom coachwork
Engine: Six cylinder T-head configuration, cast in three blocks of two each, 4½″ x 5½″ bore and stroke, 74 horsepower
Wheelbase: 133 inches
Transmission: Selective three speeds forward, one reverse, transaxle mounted
Manufacturer: Packard Motor Car Co., Detroit, Mich. (1899-1958)

1912 Packard 1-48 Victoria

The Packard, like many cars, was born from a dissatisfaction with a previous car. In this case, the car was a Winton and the customer James Ward Packard. When he complained about the performance of his car to its creator, Alexander Winton, Packard was reportedly told by the rather prickly inventor that if he thought he could build a better car then he should go and do so. Which he did. And out of that ancient taunt was born one of America's greatest marques.

Like most American builders, Packard started with small, light cars. They quickly earned a good reputation for reliability, style and performance.

In 1903, the firm moved from Warren, Ohio to Detroit and plunged foursquare into the burgeoning luxury car market, then dominated by European makes.

With its distinctive radiator shape, superb craftsmanship, spare-no-expense materials, advanced engineering and elegant style, Packard quickly became one of America's premier motorcars and continued that enviable position until World War II.

The Heritage collection's 1912 Packard is an especially stunning example of that marque's first six-cylinder models. It carries a custom-built body by Demarest & Company of New York, as ordered by Mrs. Theodate Pope Riddle, one of America's pioneer female architects who designed and founded the Avon (Conn.) School.

SPECIFICATIONS
Price new: $2,780
Engine: Straight eight flat head configuration, $3^3/_{16}''$ x 5″ bore and stroke, 120 horsepower
Wheelbase: 136 inches
Transmission: Selective three speeds forward, one reverse
Manufacturer: Packard Motor Car Co., Detroit, Mich. (1899-1958)

1933 Packard 1002 Dietrich Convertible Victoria

It's an ironic fact that Packard built some of its most stunning creations during the period 1932-1934 when its sales, like those of the entire industry, suffered from a thoroughly depressed market for new cars.

A semblance of streamlining first appeared on 1932 model Packards. This was refined in the 1933 cars to include a more deeply vee'd radiator shell, headlamp and sidelamp contours to match the radiator shell and fully skirted front and rear fenders. A generally sleeker appearance on the entire line, from the lowest priced sedan to the most lavish custom-bodied Twin Six,

was Packard's answer to Cadillac's multi-cylinder challenge.

The five passenger convertible victoria in the Heritage collection was the second most expensive model in the 1002 series Packards for 1933, exceeded in price only by the convertible sedan. The Dietrich body is a semi-custom with cowls, dashboards, windshields and numerous other items supplied stock by Packard. The rest of the coachwork was executed by Dietrich, Inc., one of the most respected names in custom auto body design and building during the glory days of the true classic car.

Despite the obvious good looks of the 1933 Packards, the year was a disaster for

sales with even those fiercely loyal to the marque holding onto their old Packards until, as the Roosevelt campaign theme song had promised, "Happy Days Are Here Again." A total of only 4800 Packards — the lowest figure since its pioneer days and the worst until its final dismal year of 1958 — were to find customers.

In light of new car prices today, it seems astonishing that a car of such value and quality as this Packard could be sold for less than $3,000 with its custom bodywork, leather interior, wire wheels, whisper-quiet straight eight and the inimitable prestige the Packard name carried.

SPECIFICATIONS

Price new: $4,300
Engine: Four cylinder T-head configuration, cast in pairs, $4^7/_8''$ x $5\frac{1}{2}''$ bore and stroke, 30 horsepower
Wheelbase: $118\frac{1}{2}$ inches
Transmission: Selective four speeds forward, one reverse
Manufacturer: Peerless Motor Co., Cleveland, Ohio (1900-1931)

1910 Peerless Model 27 Roadster

In the early days of motoring Peerless, along with Packard and Pierce-Arrow, was known as one of the "Three P's," a tribute to the high regard in which these luxury cars were held. Peerless, too, made no bones about the quality of its products, using the motto: "All That The Name Implies."

Like a number of successful auto manufacturers, Peerless had origins entirely removed from wheeled vehicles — in this case clothes wringers. It moved from there to bicycles and on to small cars powered by the ubiquitous De Dion one cylinder engines. A four cylinder car designed in 1903 by the talented and creative Louis Mooers, Peerless's chief engineer, launched the firm

into the luxury end of the business. Coupled with a long string of racing successes and speed records, at the hands of the famous Barney Oldfield, Peerless's image as a prestigious and powerful car was assured.

Heritage Plantation's beautiful Peerless, with the valet's (or mother-in-law's) seat in the rear, typifies a roadster for the elite of the day. Five glass sight gauges on the instrument panel enable the driver to monitor proper lubrication of crucial bearings, and the dual shock absorbers on each side coupled to the longitudinal and single transverse rear springs are among the many features which attest to the design and engineering quality of the automobile.

Peerless brought a six cylinder car to market in 1907 and followed Cadillac into

the V-8 world in 1916. It continued along successfully if unspectacularly through the mid-1920's when new management took the marque "down market" with a Continental-powered six cylinder car that sold in the $1500 range. The V-8 was gone by 1929, and a new line of straight eights for 1930 with highly attractive body styling by Alexis de Sakhnoffsky appeared just in time for the Wall Street crash. The company's last glorious gasp was a prototype V-16 with a sleekly handsome all aluminum body.

Peerless ceased auto production shortly after the V-16's debut and switched to a potentially more lucrative market and product: the brewing of Carlings beer and ale which it does to this day.

SPECIFICATIONS

Price new: $7,750
Engine: Six cylinder T-head configuration with dual valves, 4½″ x 5½″ bore and stroke, 48 horsepower
Wheelbase: 142 inches
Transmission: Selective four speeds forward, one reverse
Manufacturer: Pierce-Arrow Motor Car Co., Buffalo, N.Y. (1901-1938)

1919 Pierce-Arrow Model 48 Touring

Pierce-Arrow, like Peerless, had manufacturing origins far removed from transportation products. In George N. Pierce's case, the road to success began with birdcages, progressed into bicycles by 1896 and auto manufacturing by 1901, when Pierce, again like Peerless, introduced a small, light car powered by a De Dion proprietary engine. By 1904, Pierce had graduated to the luxury market with a four cylinder car called the Great Arrow. Five years later the name of the marque and the firm would change to Pierce-Arrow.

From the start, Pierce built cars of impeccable quality and workmanship, making extensive use of aluminum, bronze and

copper and in 1913, set the marque apart for decades with the introduction of its fender-mounted headlamps.

By the First World War, Pierce-Arrow's prestige stood at its pinnacle, the car choice of some of America's most prominent families and of the White House itself. Indeed, every president from Taft through F.D.R. had at least one Pierce-Arrow in the White House fleet.

Heritage Plantation's massive 1919 six-passenger touring is an excellent example of the leadership position the company enjoyed at the midpoint of its life span.

By the 1920's, however, Pierce-Arrow's charisma was beginning to falter. Its still-superb engineering was considered outdated and its styling stodgy. Moreover, it stubbornly clung to a ''six cylinders only'' policy when its competition was offering both straight and V-8 cars of more modern engineering and appearance. Pierce corrected this in 1929 with a superb straight eight and

followed through with a marvelous V-12 in 1931.

Along with the Depression, the company was battered by a short, unhappy merger with Studebaker, from which it disentangled itself in 1933 by being bought by a group of Buffalo investors after Studebaker slid into receivership.

Despite its new operating independence, sales dipped disastrously over the next few years to a trickle of 167 cars in 1937. On Friday the 13th, 1938, the firm was sold at auction bringing to a close a company which some connoisseurs believe consistently built the best cars ever produced in America.

47

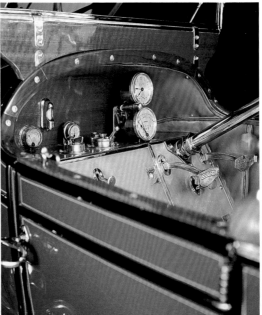

SPECIFICATIONS

Price new: $3,250
Engine: Four cylinder overhead valve configuration, 4¾″ x 5½″ bore and stroke, 50 horsepower
Wheelbase: 124 inches
Transmission: Selective four speeds forward, one reverse
Manufacturer: The Pope Manufacturing Co., Hartford, Conn. (1904-1914)

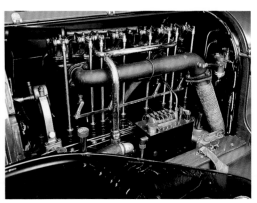

1913 Pope-Hartford Model 33 Roadster

Colonel Albert A. Pope's first bicycle was produced in 1877. Called the Columbia, it's a name which exists on bicycles to this day and in the latter part of the 19th century was the best-seller among all the high-wheelers.

By 1899, Pope had created the "bicycle trust," a collaboration of some 45 firms, just in time to see the bicycle craze fade as the new-fangled horseless carriage became the new leisure-time toy.

Pope jumped into the automaking fray with a relish reminiscent of motorcar empire builders like William C. Durant, Alfred Sloan and Henry Ford. First came the Columbia automobile in 1897, followed by the Pope-Robinson in 1903, the prestigious Pope-Toledo and the diminutive Pope-Tribune in 1904 along with the Pope-Hartford and, to round things off, the Pope-Waverly electric in the same year. Long before General Motors articulated the strategy, Col. Pope was attempting to build cars "for every purse and purpose."

The Pope-Hartford was to become the most successful and longest-lived of the Pope marques. Starting with a one cylinder car in 1904, the Pope-Hartford progressed rapidly through twins in 1905, a four in 1906 and a six in 1911. Besides earning a reputation for speed, quality and reliability as passenger cars, Pope-Hartfords enjoyed wide acceptance as a chassis for fire apparatus and commercial vehicles.

The Heritage collection's Pope-Hartford is a virtual jewel from the latter years of the brass era, and its beautiful "bright work" is complemented by the rich mahogany craftsmanship in the cockpit as well as in the cabinetry of the right side battery box. The supple leather upholstery and interior panels, fender and running board aprons further attest to the total quality of this automobile.

By the time the Heritage Pope-Hartford was built, however, the company was on its last legs with just one more year of production left. It found itself in receivership, with a product line of 18 different styles on 3 different chassis, a mix that was too large and complex for efficient manufacture. Despite rationalization into a single chassis and three body styles for 1914, the Pope automaking empire was through.

49

SPECIFICATIONS

Price new: $1,000
Engine: Horizontally-opposed two cylinder flat head configuration, 4¾″ x 6″ bore and stroke, 20 horsepower
Wheelbase: 96 inches
Transmission: Planetary two speeds forward, one reverse with final drive by single chain
Manufacturer: Reo Motor Car Co., Lansing, Mich. (1904-1936)

1909 Reo Model D Touring

ansom Eli Olds had already become a leading light in pioneer automobile manufacture with his successful curved dash Olds. He left Oldsmobile in 1904 after stockholders who held controlling interest in the company demanded that Olds abandon the curved dash in favor of more expensive and luxurious motorcars.

Olds would have none of it. He resigned to found REO, drawn from his initials, to carry on building simple, economical automobiles which gave good service and value. Indeed, that is what Reo cars would be throughout their 30-plus years of production: solid, durable and dependable transport for the American family, with only a short foray into the luxury field in the early 1930's with the fabulous Reo Royale, a stunning car which, nevertheless, racked up dismal sales.

The little one and two cylinder cars were Reo's bread and butter during its early days through 1909. The Heritage collection's Reo, authentically and beautifully restored, exemplifies those series with its engine placed "amidships fore-and-aft" so as to "distribute the weight, strain and vibration with perfect evenness," as stated in the owner's manual. Though appearing somewhat complicated to operate, with six foot pedals and three hand levers, Reo automobiles were actually relatively simple and extremely popular. In fact, sales in 1907 trailed only those of Ford and Buick in the industry.

Realizing, however, that his was becoming a dated design, R.E. Olds in 1910 introduced an F-head four cylinder car, complete with shaft drive, selective sliding gear transmission and other modern improvements necessary to stay competitive in the U.S. auto market after Ford's revolutionary Model T had arrived on the scene.

By 1912 Olds had been in the auto business for over 20 years and handed the everyday routine of Reo over to others, while retaining ownership of the firm. The conservative approach to automaking which Reo followed permitted the firm to prosper both in car and truck sales during the 'teens and twenties. With the coming of the shakeout in the industry caused by stiffer competition and fewer sales during the Depression, however, Reo closed its books on automaking during 1936. Henceforth, the company concentrated solely on the manufacture of commercial vehicles.

SPECIFICATIONS
Price new: $2,695
Engine: Straight eight flat head configuration,
3″ x 4¾″ bore and stroke, 80 horsepower
Wheelbase: 121½ inches
Transmission: Selective three speeds forward,
one reverse
Manufacturer: Rickenbacker Motor Co.,
Detroit, Mich. (1922-1927)

1925 Rickenbacker 8 Coupe

Captain Eddie Rickenbacker, a man of boundless courage who first won fame as a racing driver and then as America's flying ace of aces during World War I, was a natural to bring out after that conflict an advanced and attractive car bearing his name. His flying squadron's Hat in the Ring symbol became the Rickenbacker's emblem. The real automotive brains behind the venture, however, were Barney Everitt, William Metzger and Walter Flanders who separately and together had been involved in a number of automaking ventures since nearly the beginning of the industry.

The medium priced Rickenbacker cars, always considered mechanically innovative, came on the scene in 1922 with a six cylinder engine which had a flywheel at each end of the crankshaft to eliminate vibration once and for all. At the time, Rickenbacker was also considering offering four wheel brakes as standard equipment, but this feature would not be marketed until mid-1923.

Four wheel brakes on cars was not a new idea. Duesenberg and Kenworthy had installed them on their chassis, both of which were expensive and of limited production. Rickenbacker was the first to include them on moderately priced cars, but was subjected to a smear campaign by larger automakers who were not prepared to offer them. They absurdly claimed that this safety advance was "unsafe" because the greater braking efficiency posed the danger of throwing passengers through the windshield!

The Heritage collection's four passenger Rickenbacker represents the first year of straight eight production for the marque. It is a quality car throughout, from its eighty horsepower engine with a nine-bearing crankshaft to such amenities as "wind wings" and a pillar-mounted spotlight.

Although Rickenbacker maintained its reputation for building high-value, good-performing automobiles, the firm suffered diminishing sales in the cutthroat industry atmosphere of the mid-1920's, finally causing Rickenbacker himself to resign from the company and for production to cease early in 1927.

SPECIFICATIONS

Price new: $10,200 (chassis only)
Engine: Six cylinder flat head configuration in two blocks, 4½″ x 4¾″ bore and stroke, 40/50 horsepower
Wheelbase: 143½ inches
Transmission: Selective four speeds forward, one reverse
Manufacturer: Rolls-Royce of America, Inc., Springfield, Mass. (1921-1935)

1922 Rolls-Royce Silver Ghost, Pall Mall Phaeton

Of all cars, Rolls-Royce is surrounded by the most myths and mystique. No Rolls-Royce, for instance, has a sealed hood or a lifetime guarantee; the Parthenon-like radiator shell is not made of silver but rather, of a silver-white alloy of copper, zinc and nickel often called German silver, and the cars' sales are not limited to royalty. One claim is certainly true: for a number of years these majestic cars were built in America, initially advertised as produced by British mechanics under British supervision. But by 1924, the majority of the Springfield-built Rolls-Royce parts and systems were as American as baseball, hot dogs and you-know-what.

That the handsome American-built Silver Ghosts were equal to their British counterparts in materials and workmanship is unquestionably no myth. Each completed chassis was test-driven 100 miles. It then underwent thorough inspection and the correction of any flaws, no matter how slight, which had been noted by the driver. The approved chassis was then delivered to the coachbuilder, usually Brewster, which became a Rolls-Royce of America subsidiary in 1926.

Numerous theories have been advanced on why Rolls' American venture failed, the most persistent being that Americans who could afford Rolls-Royce cars preferred the British product. Closer to reality, perhaps, is the fact that the Silver Ghost was a magnificent, overpriced anachronism by the mid-1920's and that U.S. luxury cars had surpassed the Silver Ghost in engineering prowess, ease of operation and price advantage.

Still, the American branch built the more modern Phantom I from 1928 through 1931, and assembled and delivered some of these cars up through 1935, long after parts fabrication operations had ceased at Springfield. By that time, a total of 2,944 American Rolls-Royces had been produced.

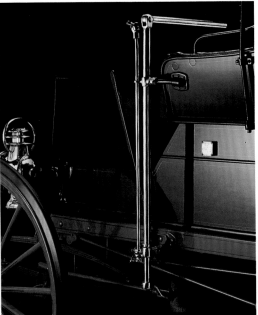

SPECIFICATIONS

Price new: $445
Engine: Horizontally-opposed air cooled two cylinder, flat head configuration, $4^{1/8}''$ x 4″ bore and stroke, 14 horsepower
Wheelbase: 87 inches
Transmission: Selective friction disc through a jackshaft to countershaft with double chain drive
Manufacturer: Sears, Roebuck & Co., Chicago, Ill. (1908-1912)

1910 Sears Model P Surrey

The great "Wish Book" for the early 20th century American family even included an automobile, and an appropriate one it was for rural motorists of the time with its hard rubber tires, high wheels and fundamental mechanism, which could be easily repaired and kept in tune by any mechanically-minded farmer.

Obviously, the Sears was not designed or meant as a town carriage for the gentry but rather as an alternative to the horse, with country-folk being loyal and stalwart customers nationwide when American roads outside the large cities consisted of two muddy tracks as the norm.

It was a mail-order car, delivered to a railroad siding much like the mail-order buggies of its time but costing more, although the Sears' exact price varied with equipment options and which issue of the Sears catalogue it was ordered from. The proud new owner would pick up his new car at the railroad point, do some basic assembly and if luck and fortune held, drive off for home with a new fangled auto buggy to take the family to church on Sunday and to do chores during the week.

The Heritage collection's Sears personifies "the surrey with the fringe on top," an excellent example of a true horseless carriage. The Sears motor buggies were well-built little cars and lived up to the byword in promotional material: "Going, Always Going." Many of the 3,500 or so customers wrote glowing testimonials: "I would not exchange this car for any $1,000 car . . ."; and in one pastor's rural ministerial work, "My running expenses are less than half the expenses of keeping a horse."

Trouble was, the great Chicago mail-order house was losing money on every car they sold and eventually got out of the auto business. Sears made another brief venture into mail-order cars in the early 1950's when they tried to sell a modified-grille version of Kaiser-Frazer's little Henry J called the Allstate, with discouraging results.

SPECIFICATIONS

Price new: $5,000 (chassis only)
Engine: Six cylinder flat head configuration,
 4³/₈″ x 6¼″ bore and stroke, 110 horsepower
Wheelbase: 144 inches
Transmission: Selective four speeds forward,
 one reverse
Manufacturer: Simplex Automobile Co.,
 New Brunswick, N.J. (1907-1924)

1916 Simplex, Crane Model 5 Touring

ften called "Crane-Simplex," these costly, ultra high-quality automobiles were built from late 1915 until 1919, then revived in 1922 and officially called Crane-Simplex at that time.

Designed by the redoubtable Henry M. Crane, the Simplex, Crane Model 5 was the descendant of the cars built under the Crane name in Bayonne, N.J. from 1912-14. Prior to that, this MIT graduate's engineering prowess had been displayed when Crane-powered speedboats won the prestigious Harmsworth Trophy no less than four times.

Simplex-Crane cars were available in chassis form only. The potential owner would thus be obliged to contract with a custom coachbuilder for the car's body, thereby sending the purchase price sometimes soaring toward the $10,000 mark, a stratospheric sum for an automobile in pre-WWI America when $25 was considered a high weekly wage.

The Heritage Simplex was the first car acquired for the collection, purchased from a Massachusetts collector/restorer in 1964. The car was originally owned by a well known Springfield, Massachusetts family.

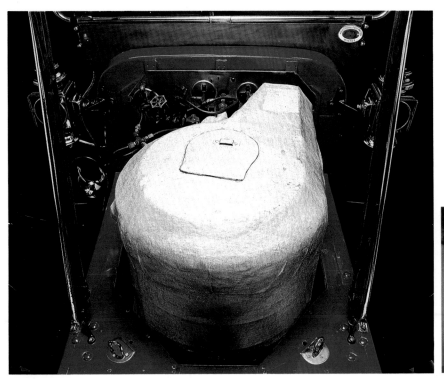

SPECIFICATIONS

Price new: $1,000
Engine: Two cylinder double acting locomotive
type, 3¼″ x 4¼″ bore and stroke,
550 lbs. steam pressure, 10 horsepower
Wheelbase: 104 inches
Transmission: None. Direct drive to rear axle
differential - no neutral
Manufacturer: Stanley Dry Plate Co., Newton,
Mass. (1897-1899); Stanley Manufacturing Co.,
Lawrence, Mass. (1899-1901); Stanley Motor
Carriage Co., Newton, Mass. (1901-1924);
Steam Vehicle Corp. of America, Newton, Mass.
(1924-1927)

1911 Stanley Steamer Model 62 Runabout

The early and the last days of Stanley steam cars were checkered ones. In between, the Massachusetts firm produced the most popular steam powered passenger cars ever built.

Created by inventive identical twins from Maine, Francis E. and Freeland O. Stanley, the first Stanley steam cars were built in 1898, and attained success virtually overnight. In 1899 the Stanleys sold their fledgling firm for $250,000, an amount considerably more than their initial investment of $20,000.

The original Stanley design went on to become the Locomobile and then the Mobile steamer. Meanwhile, the Stanley twins jumped back into the steam car business with an improved model which also found a

ready market. By 1906, when a streamlined Stanley dubbed the Woggle-Bug broke the world's land speed record at 127.66 miles per hour, the "coffin nose" Stanleys were a familiar part of the motoring scene, chuffing along in almost eerie silence compared to the loud and cantankerous gasoline-powered competition.

Popular and fast though they were, early Stanleys lacked a condenser, severely limiting their range between water refills. The Model 62's water tank under the front seat holds 28 gallons, providing only 35 to 45 miles of travel or about three-quarters of a gallon of water boil-off per mile.

By the time the Heritage collection's Stanley was built, the gasoline car held sway and steam was on its way out. White, Stanley's principal rival, had gone to

gasoline cars exclusively by that year. Self-starting systems, principally that of Cadillac also contributed to steam's demise, contrasting the near-instant starting and running of a gasoline car with the tedious, time-consuming drill needed for the Stanley to build sufficient steam pressure to run.

Stanley was caught in a game of catch-up adding electric lights, a condensing steam system which helped to extend the car's cruising range and a restyling to resemble their four-cycle gasoline competitors. Slowly and inexorably sales dwindled to a trickle and by 1923 Stanley was in receivership, its assets sold the following year to a new company which tried unsuccessfully until 1927 to carry on manufacture of the best-known steam car of all.

SPECIFICATIONS

Price new: $2,000
Engine: Four cylinder T-head configuration,
cast in pairs, 4¾″ x 5½″ bore and stroke,
60 horsepower
Wheelbase: 120 inches
Transmission: Selective three speeds forward,
one reverse integral with the rear axle
Manufacturer: Ideal Motor Car Co., Indianapoli
Ind. (1911-1913); Stutz Motor Car Co. of
America, Indianapolis, Ind. (1913-1935)

1915 Stutz Bearcat

f all American cars, the most memorably named has to be the Stutz Bearcat with its suggestion of power, endurance and speed. This is exactly what every Bearcat delivered, along with flamboyant good looks and construction nearly as rugged as the average locomotive of its time.

Ohio native Harry C. Stutz's automotive namesake got off to a stunning start in the first Indy 500 held in 1911. Taking an unproven car to that grueling contest, it finished a respectable 11th against tough competition with much larger engines. Harry Stutz, who had as much of a gift for promotion as he did for automaking, promptly dubbed his creation the "Car That Made Good in a Day."

From that time until just before World War I, Stutz indeed made good both on the

racetrack and in the showroom, offering a line of sports and touring cars of moderate price and immoderate performance. But success meant expansion and expansion meant offering stock to the public. By 1916, a stock speculator had wrested control of Stutz from Harry, who put up with this situation until 1919, then left the company he had founded to build the H.C.S. car.

By 1922, the clever speculator was broke and Stutz was taken over by Bethlehem Steel magnate, Charles Schwab, whose first significant decision was dropping the Bearcat from the line.

Better days were ahead for Stutz with the development of the Vertical Eight series in 1925. This straight eight, combined with the new Safety Chassis, again put the marque in the engineering limelight. With fabric-covered, lightweight coachwork by Weymann, the Stutz recaptured all of its old panache and became, until its demise, the

most European in concept and execution of American cars of the time.

Like all carmakers, Stutz sales faltered during the onset of the Depression. Despite a model lineup which included America's fastest production car, Stutz needed something new. In 1932 that something materialized as the sensational DV-32, an ultimate development of the Vertical Eight engine, boasting dual overhead camshafts and four valves per cylinder. Despite performance worthy of its name and a selection of custom body designs ranging from simply elegant to spectacularly sporty, the economics of the times finally overwhelmed the struggling firm which ended its motor vehicle adventure building small delivery vans called Pak-Age-Cars.

But what a ride it had been, especially at full throttle with muffler cutout wide open, in a bright yellow Bearcat like the one in the Heritage Plantation collection.

SPECIFICATIONS

Price new: $400
Engine: One cylinder overhead valve configuration, 3¼″ x 4¼″ bore and stroke, 4 horsepower
Wheelbase: 95 inches
Transmission: Friction disc via jackshaft with final dual chain drive
Manufacturer: Waltham Manufacturing Co, Waltham, Mass. (1902-1908)

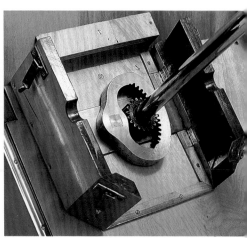

1908 Waltham-Orient Buckboard

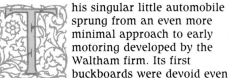

This singular little automobile sprung from an even more minimal approach to early motoring developed by the Waltham firm. Its first buckboards were devoid even of rudimentary suspension, had tiller steering, a basic little wooden body and rode on an 80 inch wheelbase. By contrast, the Heritage collection Waltham-Orient is a deluxe bit of equipage with its full elliptic springs, fenders all around to keep mud off driver and passenger, a top and an actual steering wheel. It's a tilt steering wheel at that, for a rotund driver's ease of entry, with a very quick and precise internal rack and pinion steering mechanism.

Another unusual feature is the copper-clad muffler and the exhaust system which points forward rather than exiting at the rear of the car. With the engine hung out back, Yankee pragmatism dictated the exhaust system should go forward, and there it is.

Like its buckboard predecessor the Waltham-Orient is a friction drive car. This transmission system is renowned for smooth engagement, a plethora of ratios, simplicity of concept and rapid wear accompanied by severe slippage.

In late 1908 Charles Metz took over the Waltham Company and changed the cars to his name. In the process, he created one of the first "kit" cars for which customers could order one system or package at a tim at $25 each, and assemble the required fourteen packages to complete the car und what was called the "Metz Plan." Metz retained the Orient friction drive and made it work so well that the Metz friction drive automobile found a steady market until th late 'teens.

The Waltham-Orient is one of six New England-built cars in the Heritage collectio

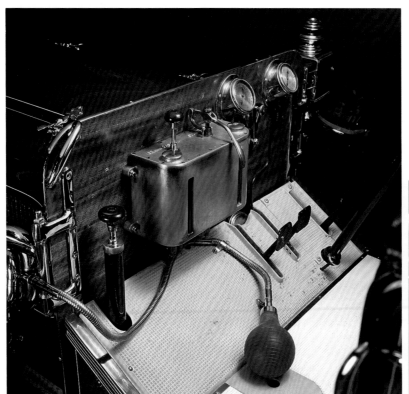

SPECIFICATIONS

Price new: $4,000
Engine: Two cylinder double acting, high pressure bore 3", low pressure bore 5"; stroke for both cylinders 4½", 40 horsepower
Wheelbase: 122 inches
Transmission: None. Shaft drive direct to rear axle two speed differential, with a neutral position
Manufacturer: The White Sewing Machine Co., Cleveland, Ohio (1900-1906); The White Co., Cleveland, Ohio (1906-1918)

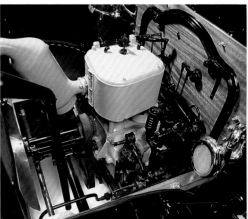

1909 White Steam Car Model M

hite was Stanley's main rival in the U.S. steam car arena and is considered to be more mechanically sophisticated than the Stanley, especially in its later years. One advance was the semi-flash boiler invented by Rollin White in the late 1890's when White first began producing cars. By 1901, 197 White Steam Cars had found buyers and the company was deep into auto manufacturing.

In 1903, the car's buggy-like appearance disappeared when the engine was moved forward under a hood and the condenser positioned up front like a radiator. The condenser recovered exhaust steam which extended the car's range to that of comparably sized gasoline engine automobiles. In 1905, the White took on its distinctive hood configuration which would carry over into its later gasoline cars and trucks. Whereas the Stanley utilizes a true boiler positioned under a hood, the White employs a steam generator mounted amidships which makes the big Model M a well-balanced, very roomy seven passenger car.

While a White had been the only automobile in Teddy Roosevelt's 1905 Inaugural Parade, the first official White House fleet of cars was ordered up by President William Howard Taft in 1909 and included the actual White Steam Car in the Heritage collection. It is indeed, a rather stately looking vehicle quite appropriate for presidential parade and touring duty. Other White owners of the time included such prominent Americans as John D. Rockefeller and Buffalo Bill Cody. The White deserved its presidential patronage for it was a car of luxury, comfort and near-silent operation.

After 1910, White concentrated on gasoline-powered cars and trucks, and from 1918 on trucks alone, after dismal sales of their big six cylinder cars drove them from the automaking end of the market.

SPECIFICATIONS

Price new: $1,500
Engine: One cylinder, horizontal configuration, variable inlet valve actuated by compressed air 5½″ x 6″ bore and stroke, 9 horsepower
Wheelbase: 69 inches
Transmission: Planetary, two speeds forward, one reverse
Manufacturer: Winton Motor Carriage Co., Cleveland, Ohio (1897-1924)

1899 Winton Motor Carriage

 f all the pioneer automotive tinkerers, dreamers and innovators, Alexander Winton was really the first successful manufacturer. A Scots immigrant who came to Cleveland in 1884, he founded the Winton Bicycle Company, then built his first experimental car in 1896.

By March, 1897 the Winton Motor Carriage Company had been organized and a year later he had sold his first car. By the end of '98, Winton had built and sold 22 cars, including one bought by James Ward Packard. It brought Packard such

dissatisfaction, that after Winton had dismissed his complaints by telling him to build a better car if he could, Packard did just that, establishing the illustrious Packard automobile.

One of Winton's production of exactly 100 cars in 1899 is in the Heritage collection. It is a "horseless carriage" in the truest sense, lacking only the hardware to hitch up old dobbin.

Like the rest of the industry, Winton made rapid technological strides in the first decade of this century building two cylinder, then four and finally, excellent six cylinder cars of solid workmanship, sound engineering and conservative design. Winton was too conservative, really, for like a number of prestigious marques, the cars lost their innovative edge and slipped into proven but

antiquated engineering and appearance after World War I. The firm relied upon loyal customers to sustain trade, but even the most loyal customer is hardly motivated to pay a premium for the same thing as years go by.

Winton, intransigent to the end and as always, convinced of his rightness in automotive design, refused to merge with any other automaker and liquidated the company in 1924. Ironically, the name of Winton lived on for a number of years as a marine diesel engine division of General Motors.

❧ Movie star Gary Cooper, original owner of Heritage Plantation's 1930 Duesenberg Model J Derham Tourster. ❧

—COPYRIGHT BY—
SCHERVEE & BUSHONG
—1910—

❧ President William Howard Taft touring in the 1909 White Steam Car, now part of Heritage Plantation's collection. ❧

INDEX

1932 Auburn	8		1912 Packard	40
1916 Brewster	10		1933 Packard	42
1910 Cadillac	11		1910 Peerless	44
1930 Cadillac	12		1919 Pierce-Arrow	46
1937 Cord	14		1913 Pope-Hartford	48
1930 Duesenberg	36, 70		1909 Reo	50
1913 Ford	7		1925 Rickenbacker	52
1915 Ford	16		1922 Rolls-Royce	54
1931 Ford	18		1910 Sears	56
1925 Franklin	20		1916 Simplex	58
1910 Knox	22		1911 Stanley	60
1927 LaSalle	24		1903 Stevens-Duryea	31
1927 Lincoln	26		1915 Stutz	62
1912 Mercer	28		1908 Waltham-Orient	64
1915 Milburn	30		1909 White	66, 71
1904 Oldsmobile	32		1899 Winton	68
1912 Oldsmobile	34			

CREDITS

Author: David Brownell
Editor: G. Robert Melber
Color Photography by: Alan Hudson
Designed, Typeset and Printed by:
On-Cape Lithographers, Inc., Hyannis, Massachusetts
Design and Layout by: Richard Vecchione